I0091503

10 Tips on How to Live a Stress-FREE Life!

By Jean Dancy

Published by InHouse Publishing
Printed in the United States of America.
Cover concept and design: Ava Monroe
Editor: Ava Monroe
ISBN: 978-0-9702779-16

To Reach Jean Dancy:
InHouse Publishing
Inhousepublishinginfo@gmail.com
Instagram: @JeanDancy

TABLE OF CONTENTS

Introduction

As you're reading this, there are people who are so stressed that it is literally *squeezing* the happiness out of them.

They're not stressed over the big things in life either. They are stressed because the line at the grocery store was too long. They are stressed because the car in front of them didn't race away at the exact second the light turned green. Let me tell you, stress makes people mean!

People can frantically flap their arms trying desperately to swim upstream---or they can get into a canoe of peace and glide smoothly over the waves of life.

We do not live in a perfect world; but we can find ways to handle this imperfect world more effectively.

Though it may not seem like it, happiness really is a choice. However, living a peaceful, stress-free life isn't an arbitrary destination where one ends up without effort. No. It takes practice and I am here to make it easy for you.

This is a simple book...filled with quick nutritious snacks that will help you live a happier, healthier life!

Choose to be happy. Choose to be peaceful. Choose to be stress-free!

The way you start your day is a great predictor of how your day will end.

Chapter One

Mornings Matter

The way you start your day is a great predictor of how your day will end. Start by spending at least the first 15 minutes--- alone. It may mean that you have to get up earlier in order to avoid the traffic in your own home.

Spend those 15 minutes praying, or practicing positive visualization. Thinking on good things that have happened in your life, or the good things that you want to happen in the future draws those good things into your life.

That time is about fueling your body and mind with a dose of something positive before anything negative has a chance to get in.

Do not wake up and grab your phone or turn on the news. Either of those actions could expose you to negative information.

Do your best to allow positive thoughts to enter your mind first.

It's easy to let the last things that we go to bed thinking about be the first things to greet us when we wake up.

However, if you wake up and say positive things every morning---your mind is programmed to go in that direction. I start my day with words of gratitude.

After your first 15 minutes, create a relaxed environment and have a delicious cup of coffee, tea, or your favorite morning drink. Listen to the kind of music that inspires you as you get dressed.

Before you leave, say at least 3 affirmations.

Example:

(1) This is going to be a great day!
(2) I was created for great things.
(3) I am loved.

Get up in enough time so that you don't have to rush to your destination. Rushing leads to the highway of stress.

Studies show that prayer actually changes things.

Dr. Caroline Leaf (a cognitive neuroscientist) says, "It has been found that 12 minutes of daily focused prayer over an 8 week period can change the brain to such an extent that it can be measured on a brain scan.

This type of prayer increases activity in brain areas associated with social interaction, compassion, and sensitivity to others."

Although studies support what I am sharing with you, I have years of experience that also attest to this. Yes, mornings matter--- so start your mornings on a positive note. That way you are much more likely to find harmony throughout the rest of your day.

Don't allow traffic to drive you crazy!

Chapter Two

Don't allow traffic to drive you crazy!

Don't just get into your car and drive somewhere arbitrarily. Buckle up and have a plan. A good plan.

Plan to show love and kindness to all of the people that you encounter in traffic. Actually plan on allowing cars to get in front of you. Pay it forward. Have positive thoughts toward the other drivers. Extend compassion. You never know what someone on the road next to you is going through. Treat them with patience as if they've just received bad news.

Don't be so quick to blow at the person who is in front of you, the person who has not moved the second after the light changes.

Don't give the finger to people or enter into any kind of adversarial exchange. When people are trying to get in front of you, in order to take the nearest exit, please slow down and allow them to exit.

I have actually seen people speed up to prevent a person from making an exit. Plan to drive in a spirit of love.

Driving in a spirit of love means that you must constantly consider what the possible circumstances are of the people around you. Some of them have just lost parents, close friends, or other relatives. Some of them have gotten terrible news from a doctor and they are on their way back from that appointment.

Treat everyone the way you would want to be treated. All it takes is practice. Instead of using curse words when people annoy you in traffic, say something nice. Example: Say, "God bless you."

Years ago a friend of mine used to be irate in traffic. I made the same suggestion to him. He promised to say, "God bless you," instead of using any profane language. The first time he tried it, he laughed so hard at himself! Though he thought it was so corny, he did it for the rest of the day and alleviated the stress that he normally felt when driving. Saying those kind words allowed him to have a better, more positive day.

Needless to say, that one decision caused him to stop allowing traffic to drive him crazy. And you can do it too!

Put a fence around your happiness and don't allow negative people inside.

Chapter 3

Put a Fence Around Your Happiness!

Your happiness has to be protected. When it is within your power---keep anything out that may disturb your happiness.

Since you know that being late for an appointment or being late to work bothers you, leave early. Arrive early with enough time to calmly collect yourself before meeting with people.

Avoid the person who always has that little negative thing to say. It sometimes feels like you've been stuck with a tiny pin---but stuck nonetheless. Run if you have to but be willing to make an abrupt departure from the person's presence.

Don't answer the phone if a negative person is calling. Answering the phone is just an invitation *not* an obligation.

Don't invite someone's negative energy into your space.

Block the person if you need to but keep the fence up around your happiness.

Don't enter into negative conversations about others either. It may seem harmless but it will deplete your happiness account.

Be diligent about putting a fence around special holidays and occasions. If you know that certain people may ruin your holiday or special moment, avoid them at all cost. Don't invite people who may disturb your peace and happiness.

We get one day a year that belongs solely to us---our birthday. You should be particularly protective about your birthday fence. Only answer the phone for the most positive people. Be careful about where you go on that day. Don't treat it like just any other day, protect it.

You want to look back on a special day or occasion and be glad you did not invite a happiness snatcher into your precious space.

Worrying is the interest you pay on negative thoughts.

Chapter 4

Don't Borrow Worry!

Never worry about something that hasn't happened yet---something that may not ever happen. That's what I call borrowing worry.

Stormie Omartian wrote a book called, "*Just Enough Light for the Step I'm on.*" I love the thought of that. It's so freeing.

If you're in school and the final test is a month away, there is no need to worry yourself sick over it before the actual test takes place. All you can do is prepare for it and do your best.

Every battle that you will ever have will first take place in your mind. Defeat the initial thought.

Like in a game of tennis, hit the negative thought away from you. A thought may come, "You will never get the job that you're interviewing for next week."

Hit that negative thought back with a positive thought and say that positive thought OUT LOUD!

That new thought could be, "I have every confidence that what's for me is for me and if that job is right for me, then I will get it. If by chance I don't get it, it's only because something greater is waiting for me."

Always have a positive outlook on things. Speak positive thoughts out boldly so that you can hear them yourself.

If you have enough light for the step that you're on---at that moment---you don't have to worry about any of the steps ahead of you.

Trying to figure future things out (often with little or no knowledge about them) can cause stress. Learning how to *not* borrow worry... may take practice. But it's totally possible. Don't borrow worry!

Until you can say "No" to others...
you will never truly be able say
"Yes" to yourself!

Chapter 5

Just Say No!

Some people find it so hard to say *no* even when they know that they don't want to do something.

Example:
You have set aside a certain Saturday to read an out of print book that you borrowed. The book has to be returned by Sunday morning. You look forward to that day with glee!

A friend calls late Friday night and says, "I need your help tomorrow. I plan to surprise my mate (who is out of town) by having our overly cluttered garage cleaned before he or she returns Sunday morning. I realize that I can never finish it alone. I need some help to finish. So will you help me clean our garage tomorrow? We need to start very early."

You know immediately that you do not want to help clean the garage. What would you do? Your answer will say a lot about how you value your time and how you deal with things that you don't want to do.

People who find it hard to say *no* are called "People pleasers." They constantly vote against themselves in an effort to be liked by others. Then they complain about how they are always doing something for someone else. They can give you a list longer than an ancient scroll of all the things they have to do for everybody else. That list then becomes the reason why they no longer have any time for themselves.

If this description sounds like I'm talking about you, you may want to consider what I'm about to say.

When you love yourself enough, and you are no longer looking for something outside of yourself---to validate you---your behavior will change. How you treat yourself will always mirror how you feel about yourself.

If you do not have a proper fence around your life, you will be open for people to come in and try to take advantage of you and your time.

The first step in the right direction...is to be true to yourself. Always honor how you *really* feel in every situation. It's never too late to change!

Making constant withdrawals from your life---without making enough deposits---can leave you empty.

Chapter 6

Take Time for Yourself!

Some people say they don't have any time for themselves. You are in control of your time, how you spend it, and how you allow other people to spend it.

You're much like a bank, in that people are constantly making deposits or withdrawals from you.

Constant withdrawals of time from a person without sufficient deposits will deplete a person. People can also be depleted spiritually, emotionally, and physically.

To the people who say that they have no time for themselves, I say this: YOU are the one, the---ONLY ONE---in control of your time.

You are the manager of your own life. Therefore you are the only one who can decide to make a change. People who don't take time for themselves often feel pressed and stressed.

Though they are sometimes unaware of it, they may feel less important than others.

I love the *VIP method.* Choose the MOST special or important people in your life. Those are the people who will have special access to you---the people who will receive special attention and special privileges from you. Only giving your most valuable time and effort to a select few people allows you to be in a surplus and not depleted from *spreading yourself too thin.*

Taking time for yourself can start with very small increments. You can take ten minutes out of your day to enjoy doing something that's just for you. You could savor a delicious treat, you could read, or check on a friend. You could even do as my daughter does. She loves to take long showers while listening to her favorite music. A friend of mine has his favorite pastry each morning with a delicious cup of coffee. When he treats himself that way he says the world is right... all right.

Looking forward to an evening bath can do wonders for you.

Anything that allows you to stop, regroup, and honor yourself is worth it. You simply must take time for yourself if you want to be stress-free!

Live life on purpose...with a purpose.

Chapter 7

Live Life on Purpose

You can decide to live your life giving love, kindness, and genuine compliments, and consideration to others. Life is so much easier and happier that way. I call it living the love life---living life on purpose. Imagine leaving home everyday with the intention of pouring as much love, kindness, and understanding on people as you possibly can. It's an exciting way to live!

While driving, you will actually look for people who are on the side trying to get over in traffic; and you will allow those people to get over. In the grocery store, you will be the one who allows the person with only one item to get in front of you. You will see an elderly lady who just got her hair done---and you will go out of your way to compliment her.

Look for beautiful things and speak about them. My mother taught me to do that.

Don't lie though. Never do that. Only say what you really feel.

Go to work with the intention of doing the best job that you're capable of doing. Go with the intention of being kind and helpful to everyone---no matter how they treat you. It takes an enormous amount of strength to be kind to rude people but it is so rewarding. Each time you do that, you're saying, "I am in control of my actions and I will not live my life---according to what you choose to say to me." You are choosing *not* to give your power away to other people.

You get to sit behind the driver in traffic who doesn't move the second after the light changes---and decide to give the driver a moment. Refuse to blow the horn right away. You don't know why the driver seems slow at that moment. It could be an elderly person who could become nervous if you blew the horn too quickly. The person could have just received terrible news. Decide to extend grace.

The point is this: Living the love life and living life on purpose are stress-free ways of living.

They bless the world and they also bless you!

Every time you speak, you are either building something negative or something positive.

Chapter 8

Watch What You Say!

Words are like building blocks. Every time you speak, you are building something negative or something positive. One of the easiest ways to bring stress into your life... is with words. It takes the same amount of time to say something positive as it does to say something negative.

Negative talk brings negative things. A lady in the grocery store said, "Just like clockwork, I get a really bad cold at this time every year." What she did not know is that she is the one who schedules her cold---with her words. If she were to break out of that mindset and declare, "I will not get another cold at this time of year. In fact, I will not get a cold at all this year,"---her reality would start changing in order to match her words.

The person who says the following words will likely get a predictable result. "I'm up for another promotion this year and I know that I will not get it.

I've been interviewed for this position for the last three years and I didn't get it. I know I won't get it this year either." That person is much more likely not to get the promotion.

If there are two people up for the same promotion and both are equally qualified, the person who speaks positively is much more likely to get it.

Words either tilt things in our favor or tilt the odds against us. Therefore it pays to practice positive speaking all the time.

Be willing to have people look at you strangely when you break out of the norm in terms of what you say. I can sneeze and someone will say, "Oh, I see you're catching a cold." I will speak up immediately and say, "No, I'm not catching a cold. A cold may be trying to catch me."

You shouldn't say negative things like, "I'm so stupid, I'm so clumsy, and I'm an idiot." Those are statements that put you down... especially if they're said by you.

You are creating the world around you with your words.

Your voice is the most important audible voice that you hear, so be kind to yourself. Be the loudest cheerleader on your team. Never root against yourself. The more positive energy you create around yourself---the more positive results you will see. You are the only *you* that you have, so treat yourself accordingly.

Dare to live your best life and allow your words to give you the proper foundation on which to stand.

Order is one of the foundations of peace.

Chapter 9

Have a Place for Everything!

There are people scurrying around right now looking for their car keys. The longer it takes to find them, the more stressful it becomes. When there are things in our lives that cause stress, it is wise to eliminate those things by finding solutions to them immediately.

People who misplace keys frequently can hang them on the wall inside of their homes or find other solutions that may work. Though you may not know it, the simple things that appear harmless are the ones that mount up daily.

A friend looked through her cabinet trying to locate the hot sauce to pour into a pot on the stove. My first thought was, "Why don't you have a place for the hot sauce?"

You don't have to be like a certain lady I know (wink, wink!). In her home, the hot sauce is in the cabinet directly to the right of her stove.

It is on the second shelf all the way on the left side.

She has a specific place for everything. You don't have to go that far but at least everything could have its own shelf. It would make navigating the kitchen a much more pleasurable experience.

I've seen people search for receipts with no idea where they are. Looking for things can be annoying and literally irritating. Look for areas of potential stress and find solutions for them.

For papers, a file box works well. Buy some labels and do something like this: House Related, Insurance, Personal Information, etc.

If that seems a bit daunting right now and you are not super organized, you can simply get a big bag for important papers, a bag for all receipts, and a bag for all miscellaneous papers. Label the bags and live a more peaceful life.

Even have a place for your thoughts. Yes, your thoughts.

If it is January and there is something stressful that you need to do in June, refuse to think about it ahead of time. Your brain works for you. You decide what it thinks. When that "June thought" comes, have another thought right there waiting to take its place. Have a Bible scripture or a lovely quote that you can say whenever that thought comes to your mind.

Thoughts about past failures and things that you should have done often vie for your attention. For example, you always planned to finish college but you did not. Just when you think you're having a great day---BAM! You're hit with that thought again. Arrest it. Handcuff it right there at the front door of your mind and stop it from moving any closer.

Either make peace with and totally accept the fact that you did not finish college---or find a way to go back to school. Either way, put that thought in its place.

Refuse to ride the marry-go-round of stress... doing the same stressful things day in and day out. Get off of the marry-go-round and relax. Enjoy peace...and live a stress free life!

How you see life is how you experience life!

Chapter 10

How You See Life

How you see life is how you experience life. Life has an amazing way of becoming---for you---what you see and what you expect.

Expectancy brings things. Expect good things and you are far more likely to get them. Expect bad things and you are far more likely to get bad things.

Know that you are a co-creator of all that happens to you. Look at it this way. Remember the seesaw on the playground when you were younger? One side would usually be up and the other side would be down.

When it comes to life's "Seesaw," you determine whether it is up for you or down for you.

Perception is key.

In a situation, are you more likely to see the glass half full or half empty?

Example:

You've been on a job 10 years. The manager walks into the office of 20 people and announces, "We are going to have to let at least 10 people from this office go by the end of the month."

Which of the following thoughts is more likely yours?

(A) I don't believe that I will be one of the people that they let go. But if I am, when one door closes another one opens.

(B) I know they are going to let me go. What on earth will I do?

The person in example (A) had optimistic thoughts. That person saw the glass half full. The person in example (B) had pessimistic thoughts and saw the glass half empty. Given the same circumstance, one person saw the glass half full and another one saw the glass half empty.

Life is such that each thought caused the seesaw to move in one direction or the other. The optimistic person (because of his or her own thoughts), is more likely the one who gets to keep the job.

Thoughts give out either positive or negative energy. Although the manager may not be aware of it (assuming that all of the workers are on the same level), the people who have negative energy are more likely to be the ones who are chosen to leave.

Life is choice driven, which means that you get to choose how you think. It doesn't matter how long you've been a negative thinker, you may freely choose to become a positive thinker today! It takes time but it gets easier with practice. Soon you could have positive thoughts flowing effortlessly through your mind.

Start right now!

Question and Answer

Question: Why did you write this book?

Answer: I wrote this book because I have gotten the same question from people---all of my life, "Why are you so happy?" Even as a teenager, I tried to pinpoint exactly why I was so happy all the time.

Question: Did you get an answer?

Answer: Yes, actually I did. It wasn't that things went smoothly all the time in my life. It was how I chose to react to those things that made the difference.

Question: How did you choose to react?

Answer: Looking back, I always chose to see the glass half full---rather than half empty. I would gravitate immediately to whatever good I could get from a situation.

Question: Can you give me some examples?

Answer: Yes, I was a good student...an honor student.

Question and Answer Continued...

But if I received a lower grade than I expected, I chose to get happy about the grade I would get next. I knew it was a temporary situation; and I shouldn't spend any time moaning over spilled milk.

I remember when I taught high school English. On the first day of school I told my 10th graders, "I am in a very happy mood today. And this is the mood that I will have everyday for the rest of the year. I will never be in an angry or grumpy mood. Ever!"

Of course the teenagers were amazed by my statement. Everyday one young man would rush to my room, see my smile, and say, "Yes, you're in a good mood *again* today."

That statement was an easy one for me to make because I determine my own mood. I don't allow circumstances to toss me back and forth.

Students did things that could have caused me to become angry; but I didn't think that their actions should have the power to override the decision that I made for my life.

Question: How do you think this book will help people?

Answer: This book gives them a quick and practical guide to living a happier, stress-free life.

I give clear and simple examples of how to react in a positive way to many different stressful situations.

Living a stress-free life is definitely linked to living a longer life. It is also among the best things you can do for your health.

We, as people, have the power to choose our moods. And I choose to be happy. Happiness really is a decision and it starts with YOU!

About the Author

Muhammad Ali fascinated a little girl with his fancy footwork in the ring and caused her to fall in love with the sport of boxing. Her biggest dream was to meet Ali. Though destiny had something even better in mind. That little girl was Jean Dancy.

Author of the poem "My Black King," the Alabama A&M University graduate is grateful to have worked as an Actress, Model, Make- up Artist, Jazz Singer, English Teacher, Sportswriter, Motivational Speaker, Life Skills Teacher, Real Estate Broker, and Certified Mediator.

However, Dancy made Boxing history when she became the only woman to become both a Boxing Manager and a Boxing Promoter. Additionally, Jean is the first female to manage and later promote an athlete who was also her husband. Under Dancy's management, Marty Monroe soared to a #4 world ranking in the Heavyweight boxing division.

Throughout her career, Dancy has received recognition for her achievements. Some of those achievements include being named "Woman of the Year" in sports for her accomplishments in the boxing business and being honored for becoming a member of the multi-million dollar circle of salespeople as a Real Estate Broker.

What about Muhammad Ali?—and destiny?

Jean didn't just meet Ali, she became the only female boxing manager in his Deer Lake Training Camp! Jean has written about her experiences in camp and her friendship with Muhammad in the riveting book, "Muhammad Ali and Me."

As a Sportswriter, and boxing enthusiast, Dancy has connected with some of the most elite boxers, trainers, and promoters in the history of the sport. That list includes Muhammad Ali, Joe Frazier, George Foreman, Don King, Evander Holyfield, Thomas "Hit Man" Hearns, Roberto Duran, the Mayweathers, and many more.

Jean Dancy, the mother of a lovely daughter named Ava, particularly enjoys helping people in relationships, motivational speaking, singing, and painting.

"Muhammad Ali and Me"
By Jean Dancy

THERE IS NO bigger name or icon on planet Earth than Muhammad Ali (among mere human beings); and despite the odds, God allowed my footsteps to meet at the same place...and at the same time...with his footsteps.

My biggest dream—in life—was to meet Ali, but God had something far greater in mind.

This is the story of a little girl who wanted to meet Muhammad Ali...the lengths she took on that journey...and what happened when her dream finally came true.

Available at Amazon, Barnes and Noble, and online everywhere books are sold.

To Reach Jean Dancy:

InHouse Publishing
Inhousepublishinginfo@gmail.com
Instagram: @JeanDancy

www.ingramcontent.com/pod-product-compliance
Lightning Source LLC
Chambersburg PA
CBHW072155020426
42334CB00018B/2015